Tallahassee Homeowner's Guide To Selling Your Home

HOW TO SELL YOUR HOME FAST, FOR
TOP-DOLLAR, IN FLORIDA'S CAPITAL CITY

Jason Picht, Realtor®

TALLAHASSEE, FLORIDA

Copyright © 2014 by Jason Picht.

All rights reserved. No part of this publication may be reproduced, distributed or transmitted in any form or by any means, including photocopying, recording, or other electronic or mechanical methods, without the prior written permission of the publisher, except in the case of brief quotations embodied in critical reviews and certain other noncommercial uses permitted by copyright law. For permission requests, write to the author.

Jason Picht
1530 Metropolitan Blvd
Tallahassee, FL 32308
www.jasonpicht.com

Tallahassee homeowner's guide to selling your home / Jason Picht. —1st ed.
ISBN 978-1502752871

Contents

The #1 Most Important Factor If You Want To Sell Your Home Fast, For Top-Dollar! 1

Creating 2006-like Bidding Wars Today! 3

How To Find The Right Price 5

Other Important Factors You Need To Know 7

    Fixes and Updates Keep Money In Your Pocket 8

    Set The Stage To Sell 8

The 15 Golden Questions: Don't Hire A Realtor® Until You Ask These Questions 11

The 14 Factors Buyers Are Using To Judge Your Home. 15

    Curb appeal 16

    Functionality 18

    Livability 23

    The High Cost Of Ignoring What Buyers Want 27

How To Make Your Home One Of The 40+ I Sell This Year 29

To Megan,
Thank you for being my helpmate. Thank you for loving me, respecting me, supporting me, encouraging me, and believing in me even when I didn't believe in myself. I love you.

Under all is the land. Upon its wise utilization and widely allocated ownership depend the survival and growth of free institutions and of our civilization. Realtors should recognize that the interests of the nation and its citizens require the highest and best use of the land and the widest distribution of land ownership. They require the creation of adequate housing, the building of functioning cities, the development of productive industries and farms, and the preservation of a healthful environment. Such interests impose obligations beyond those of ordinary commerce. They impose grave social responsibility and a patriotic duty to which Realtors should dedicate themselves, and for which they should be diligent in preparing themselves. Realtors, therefore, are zealous to maintain and improve the standards of their calling and share with their fellow Realtors a common responsibility for its integrity and honor. In recognition and appreciation of their obligations to clients, customers, the public, and each other, Realtors continuously strive to become and remain informed on issues affecting real estate and, as knowledgeable professionals, they willingly share the fruit of their experience and study with others.

--excerpt from the preamble to the Realtor Code of Ethics

Dear Reader,

This little book is my effort to share with you the fruit of my experience and study. I hope that it will help you better understand how to sell your home quickly and for top dollar!

To your success,

Jason

PART 1

The #1 Most Important Factor If You Want To Sell Your Home Fast, For Top-Dollar!

One word...Price.

OK...I know that may have been obvious to you when you read it, but A LOT...I mean A LOT of homeowners know it, but don't "get it."

The #1 mistake I see homeowners make is pricing their home too high in this market because they think the market is back to where it was in 2006. It's not! When you price too high, you end up chasing the market...always a little behind it...never able to catch up.

That's what causes those nightmare stories you've heard from your neighbors and co-workers who've had to wait 12, 18, even 24 months or more to sell their home. On the contrary, I just listed a house last week and have had seven showings already (and one offer). My client told me that we've had more showings on her house in a week than her friend has had in six months!

Whether you choose to hire me to sell your home, hire another Realtor® or sell it yourself, I don't want you to have to suffer through that particular nightmare.

I wouldn't wish that fate on my worst enemy.

If you are serious about selling your home and getting that next DREAM HOME at today's fabulous prices (and still once-in-a-lifetime low interest rates) you've got to be real about pricing your home to sell.

Unfortunately, you might not get what you want for it, but you'll get every penny of what it's worth.

Keep an eye on your bigger goal: Living where you want in the home that's perfect for you and your family.

PART 2

Creating 2006-like Bidding Wars Today!

A funny thing happens when you price your home just ahead of the market...
The market recognizes value and jumps on it. In fact, I'm seeing mini-bidding wars erupt over good homes with the right starting price the day they hit the market.

Some are even selling for more than the listing price! Case in point...In 2012, my wife Megan and I bought a home. It came on the market at a bargain price, which attracted buyers. It got competitive and we ultimately paid above the listing price to get our "dream home". And we couldn't be happier...it was the right home at a tremendous value.

PART 3

How To Find The Right Price

The very first thing I do with my clients is work on pricing. My goal is to sell my clients' homes for the HIGHEST possible price in the SHORTEST possible time.

Having a home sit on the market "wishing" for a higher than market price ALWAYS, ALWAYS, ALWAYS causes you to lose money.

If you work with me, or work with another professional, PLEASE listen to the advice they are giving you about price. You should be working with a Realtor® who's sold a significant number of homes in this market.

Pricing in this market is way more difficult than pricing homes in 2004, 2005 and 2006.

Not only should your Realtor® be looking at "comps" (similar homes that have recently sold), but they also need to have a feel for the micro-market in your part of town.

There's no magic formula for pricing, the best thing you can do is get the advice of a professional.

PART 4

Other Important Factors You Need To Know

Most Realtors® will tell you "Location, Location, Location" and yes, location is important in selling your home, but there's not much you can do to improve your location...unless you can put your home on a trailer and haul it across town.

So let's focus on the things you can control.

Condition...

The condition of your home is critical. If you've got a few nagging things to fix, fix them.

If your kitchen or bathrooms need updating, consider doing the updates before you list your home.

I help my clients assess their home and identify what needs to be fixed or updated, how much to spend and how it will affect the home's price.

Fixes and Updates Keep Money In Your Pocket

In the old days (like 2000-2006) adding updates to your home added value, but most of the time weren't necessary to sell it.

Today, buyers know they've got lots of options and they don't want to buy your home and then renovate it. They want "move-in ready."

In fact, the trend I'm seeing is that buyers are penalizing sellers for not doing updates and repairs...to the tune of $2 to $1. Meaning a repair or update that might cost $1000 if you pay for it and have it done before you sell, will cost you $2000, or possibly even $3000, in the sale price if you pass it on to the buyer to take care of.

It's usually in your interest to have the work done before you sell. But before you do any work on your home call me at (850) 251-6643 or email me at jasonpicht@gmail.com.

I'll be happy to help you decide what changes are needed and how much (max) to spend.

Set The Stage To Sell

Staging, staging, staging...it's been all the rage since waaaayyy back in the 1990's and for a very good reason. Staged homes sell.

Most buyers decide within the first 30 seconds of entering your home if it's right for them. If they walk in and see a cluttered mess, they aren't buying.

You've got to make it easy for buyers to picture themselves living in your home. And don't rely on their imagination...you'll be sorely disappointed!

PART 5

The 15 Golden Questions: Don't Hire A Realtor® Until You Ask These Questions

If you're thinking about hiring a Realtor® to sell your home (and you should)...there are some things you need to know BEFORE you hire them. This is not that time to hire your mom's best friend Janice who's a part-timer (when she's not playing Bridge).

It's really important that you find someone that's a "fit" for you. Here are what I call the 15 "Golden Questions" that will help you get to know the Realtors® you're considering.

#1. How long have you been a licensed Realtor®? *There are new Realtors® hanging out their shingle every day...make sure you're getting someone with experience.*

#2. Do you work full-time as a Realtor®? *The overwhelming majority of Realtors® in Tallahassee are part-time. Do you want a part-timer or would you better served by a full-time professional?*

#3. Do you have assistants that work for you? *Find out if you'll be passed off to one or more assistants...or if you will you get personal attention from the Realtor®.*

#4. How many homes did you list last year that sold? *This will tell you if the person can sell at all.*

#5. How many homes did you list last year did not sell? *This will tell you if they are selling most of the homes they list.*

#6. How many of the listings you took did you sell yourself? *If possible, find a Realtor® who is selling at least 10-20% of his or her own listings...this means they're doing a good job of finding buyers for the homes they list.*

#7. How many transactions did you do last year? *Look for a Realtor® that is selling several homes a month (minimum).*

#8. What was your average list price to sales price ratio for your listings? *This will tell you how well the Realtor® is at getting the price right at the start.*

#9. What is the Tallahassee Board of Realtors average list price to sales price ratio? *This will give you an indication of how your Realtor® did vs. all the other Realtors® in Tallahassee.*

#10. **What is the average number of days your listings are on the market?** *This will tell you how long it takes your Realtor® to sell homes on average.*

#11. **What is the average number of days all listings are on the market, reported by the Tallahassee Board of Realtors?** *This will give you an indication of how your Realtor® did vs. all the other Realtors® in Tallahassee.*

#12. **Where do you advertise your listings and how often?** *Make sure you're getting good placement on the Internet...that's where buyers start looking. What offline marketing will be done?*

#13. **How do you communicate with sellers and how often can I expect to hear from you?** *This is <u>VERY IMPORTANT</u>...once you list your home you should get a call from your Realtor® at least weekly, and more often when your home is being shown.*

#14. **How often do you analyze the market and pricing?** *The market changes daily as new homes, more foreclosures and the national economy affect real estate prices. Make sure you get a Realtor® that's monitoring the changes weekly.*

#15. **Why should I hire you?** *If the Realtor® you're interviewing can't sell you on why you should hire them, how will they sell your home?*

PART 6

The 14 Factors Buyers Are Using To Judge Your Home

You never get a second chance to make a first impression. Nowhere, perhaps, is this more critical to understand than in real estate. We can easily think of numerous scenarios where the first impression is a key indicator of success. A first date, an initial job interview, or a tryout for a sports team are all common experiences where we innately know that if we fail on the first attempt, then our chances of success are greatly diminished. Selling a house is much the same, but the stakes are much higher.

A buyer's first impression of your home is critical, and it happens on many levels. I have developed a detailed process that I work through to evaluate your home for its "sell-ability." Throughout this process, thinking like a buyer is essential!

Curb appeal

Curb appeal refers to the exterior presence of a home and its architecture, beauty, charm, and detail. It also refers to the initial impression of the home and whether or not it feels "inviting." Moreover, how well a home is taken care of on the exterior can say a lot about how well (or not well) a home is most likely maintained on the interior. As such, it can immediately either draw a person to a home, or repel them from it. Curb appeal includes:

1. Grounds and driveways

Driveways are checked to see if they are cracked or crumbling; I look for any signs of erosion, pooling water, or water runoff; slope is also considered; grounds are checked for signs of lawn health -- are there different types of grass that make for an unsightly appearance? Are there excessive weeds or bare spots in the lawn? Trees are considered; do they appear to be in good health? Are limbs drooping or damaged? Do limbs oversail the roof? Is there an excessive amount of leaves and debris on the roof because of trees? If so, how has that affected the roof's appearance and longevity? What is the condition of plants and bushes? Do these contribute to or take away from curb appeal? Are there any easy or inexpensive fixes to improve curb appeal?

2. Windows and doors

Do windows and doors appear to be in good condition? Are windows original to the home? Are windows made of wood? Are they single or double-paned? Are windows operational? Do doors open and close properly? Do they appear outdated in their style or detailing? Windows and doors are checked to see if any cracks appear above their corners. This is one of the most common places for cracks as a result of foundation damage to appear; cracks in these places necessitate further investigation into settling and/or foundation damage.

3. Siding and exterior paint

Siding is examined to determine its type; special care is given to homes built in the 80's and 90's to see if these homes have LP (Louisiana Pacific) or EIFS (synthetic stucco) exterior because these exterior finishes can potentially have significant problems. Masonite, LP, and hardie board can all look very similar. Thickness and texture of the siding is felt to ascertain which siding is present in the case at hand; hardie board is much more desirable than LP or masonite and this affects value and insurance prices. Paint condition is assessed to check for signs of peeling or chalking as these decrease value. Paint color is determined to have a positive, neutral, or negative effect on sellability. Brick exterior is especially desirable, but can have its own problems. If brick is present, it is checked for cracks in the bricks and mortar joints (especially around windows and doors).

4. Lot size, slope, and orientation

Lot size is an important component of valuing real estate. Is the lot size appropriate for the neighborhood? A lot that is too small or too large can detract from value. Lot size is especially affected by the law of diminishing marginal returns. Each additional increment of acreage (determined by the neighborhood and market) is worth less than the previous increment. Lot slope is also very important as it determines usability. Some lots are so severely sloped that they have little to no usability (utility). Severe slope toward the house can create significant water intrusion concerns. Water intrusion can lead to rot, rust, corrosion, mold, mildew, and a host of other problems. These issues must be remedied prior to putting a home on the market for sale. Location and orientation of the lot are assessed for traffic volume, access to the frontage road, and sunlight. Lots fronting high traffic roads are less valuable unless they are very large (in which case the major road frontage may actually add value). Flag lots are less valuable. Lots that are oddly shaped (not square or rectangular) can also be less valuable.

Functionality

Functionality refers to the main physical, structural, and mechanical components of a home that make it suitable and habitable for human occupancy. Functionality can be thought of as the "bones" of the home. This portion of the pre-listing process is the most important to get right if funds are limited and other areas of concern cannot be addressed. The reason for this is two-fold. First, buyers can sometimes overlook deficiencies in other areas so long as a home "has good bones" and it is priced accordingly. Second, and even more importantly, items 5-8 below directly impact the insurability of a house. If any of those items has a major defect, then a home will not be insurable. If a prospective buyer cannot obtain homeowner's insurance, then his or her bank will not loan money on the purchase of the home. If a borrower cannot obtain financing, then the pool of potential buyers is dramatically reduced as are the seller's proceeds from the home and the possibility of selling it at all. Functionality includes:

5. Foundation

The foundation is examined to determine its type -- slab or crawlspace, on grade or off grade; if there is a stem wall, then it is checked for foundation vents. If vents are present, then the house has a crawl space. Extra attention is then given to potential water intrusion under the home as this can cause fungus and woodrot that can damage the structural integrity of the house. If no foundation vents are present in the stem wall, then the foundation is a monolithic slab on backfilled dirt inside the stem wall. Stem wall is checked for cracks, especially those which are greater than 1/4" in width or staggered in depth (front-to-back). Cracks that are staggered front-to-back where the block seems to be depressed into, or coming out from, the face of the stem wall can be especially problematic. This holds true for brick as well. On the other hand, stepwise cracks are relatively common and usually not a cause for concern if they are small. If slab is on grade, then the distance from the slab to base plate is checked. 8-12 inches from grade level to base plate is preferred to avoid woodrot -- both of the structural dimension lumber and the siding and/or sheathing (depending on siding type). Walking through the interior of the home can uncover whether settling has occurred which can indicate foundation problems depending on its severity. A pre-listing home inspection is recommended if any problem indicators are present or if the home is over 40 years old.

6. Roof

The roof is one of the most expensive components of a home, and it is vital to protecting the home from water intrusion. It is also one of the most visible parts of a home, so it is an especially important part of selling a property. The roof is first examined to determine its type. Asphalt shingle is the predominant roof covering and it comes in two main types -- architectural and 3-tab. The architectural shingle is highly preferred for its added wind protection (because it is heavier and has two layers), durability, and aesthetic appeal (due to a dimensional appearance and color variation). 3-tab shingles detract from value in all but the lowest price ranges (under $100,000) due to their basic appearance and "economy" look. Metal roofs are the second most common roof covering in Tallahassee. The standing seam variety is preferable because it is essentially a lifetime roof and is almost impenetrable to leaks. The "tuff-rib" type of metal roof is attractive but has historically had problems with its fasteners (they are exposed and can rust...although manufacturers are working on correcting this defect on new tuff-rib roofs). Metal roofs look best on a cabin or craftsman style home and, despite their durability, can be a detriment to curb appeal in some instances. Other types of roof covering (e.g. barrel tile, green roofs, etc) are very rare in Tallahassee, but these are considered. Roof slope/pitch is also evaluated for compatibility with the roof covering type.

7. HVAC

The heating and cooling system is generally the second most expensive single component of a home. The system is examined to determine its approximate age if the exact age is not known by the seller. System brand is checked and graded (high-end, middle, or builder grade). Systems older than 10 years may be nearing the end of their useful life if they have not been well maintained. However, top end systems (Carrier or Trane) can easily last 20+ years with proper maintenance. SEER (seasonal energy efficiency ratio) is also checked. SEER ratings above the code minimum (13) add value. System type (mini-split, split system, or package system) is evaluated; ductwork location is also noted. Ductwork located under a home can cause moisture problems in the crawl space. When ductwork is present in a crawlspace, special attention is given to wood floors (if applicable) to see if they have buckled at all. If so, there may be problems with the ductwork and/or lot drainage.

8. Electrical and plumbing

One of the major advances of the 20th century that increased our quality of life tremendously was indoor plumbing and electricity becoming a standard part of every home. Plumbing materials have varied over the years, and some types (like polybutylene) are especially prone to leaks and should be replaced prior to listing. Cast iron and galvanized steel will rust from the inside out, and these need to be monitored for signs of decay. The waste disposal system of a home can be connected to a public sewer or an on-site septic tank. Many misconceptions about septic tanks abound, so it necessary to determine which type of system is present and its condition. Regarding electrical, some types of wiring (like knob and tube) are unsafe and ought to be replaced prior to listing. Other times, the breaker panel itself may be known to have defects that affect safety or insurability. These items need to be addressed as well. Moreover, the size (amperage) of the electrical service to a home will be checked to make sure it is adequate to handle the current load of the house. While a 100 or 150 amp panel may have been sufficient to handle the electrical needs of yesteryear, they are no longer sufficient to handle the electrical power requirements of a modern home (unless it's quite small). If a home does have 150 amp service or less, then it should have most or all of its major appliances and systems running on natural gas (e.g. clothes dryers, furnaces, hot water heaters, and ranges & ovens).

9. Floor plan and layout

A home can live either much larger or much smaller than its actual square footage. Most buyers currently prefer an "open" floor plan which means that there are no walls dividing the main living spaces (living room, kitchen, and dining room) from one another. Large or awkwardly placed hallways can eat up square footage and make a home less usable. Special attention is given to where furniture is or could be placed and how occupants would generally walk through a space. If furniture placement causes a house to be choppy, then that can usually be fixed easily with better staging. However, if room placement makes a house choppy, then this detracts from value. Whether or not a home is a split-plan or split-level (these are different) is considered in determining value. Split-level homes are very undesirable in today's market. Split-plans are most desirable for homes where the target buyer is a family with children who are out of elementary school.

Livability

Livability refers to the comfort and ease with which a home can be occupied. It can be associated with the feeling that makes a house into a home. While personal decorations, family photos, and the actual occupants of a house themselves are essential to a house "being a home", the factors below are no less critical in that respect. Livability includes:

10. Room sizes

The sizes of rooms determine their usability. Rooms can be too big or too small depending on which room they are and how large they are relative to the size of the home. Rooms can also be so large or small as to become unusable or awkward. It is generally better to have three good sized bedrooms rather than four extremely small bedrooms. 13x11 or 12x12 bedrooms

(143-144 sq ft) are commonly considered to be the minimum desirable size. For ancillary (non-master aka children's/guest's) bedrooms, these are very satisfactory. Ideally, a master bedroom will be able to fit a queen size bed with two end tables and a chest-of-drawers or hope chest comfortably. 15x11 or 14x12 (165-168 sq ft) is about the minimum acceptable size unless the home is much older (in which case, smaller bedrooms are expected). Living rooms, dining rooms, and kitchens are assessed for their size, layout, and positioning with respect to one another. The "work triangle" (refrigerator, sink, and stove) is particularly important. "Galley kitchens" are undesirable in most cases.

11. Flooring type and style

Flooring is an important aspect of a home as it adds color and can add or detract from a home's warmth. Flooring is one of the ways that homeowners can express their style and individuality. As such, flooring can either be a benefit or detriment to selling a home depending on how loud or bold the flooring choice is and whether or not it is currently in style. Since it is constantly underfoot, all flooring is subject to significant wear and tear. All flooring needs to be replaced or refinished in time. Badly stained or worn flooring will detract from a home's appeal and can quickly distract a potential buyer by making an entire home feel dirty or "gross". Wood floors are determined to be real or engineered. Real hardwood floors are universally desirable. Carpet is generally acceptable in bedrooms, but not elsewhere (except in lower price ranges). The main question when it comes to flooring is: Is it clean, well maintained, and in style?

12. Paint colors

Paint is the other main way that homeowners can express their style and personality. It is also the main way that parents allow their children to express their personality and changing likes and desires. Paint can make a home feel open, bright, airy, warm, and inviting (good things) or closed in, cold, dreary, and uninviting (bad things). Fortunately, paint is relatively easy and inexpensive to change if needed. Most homeowners object to painting for this very reason, but the reasons listed above that affect a home's feel are the reasons to paint, if needed. It is important to remember in this category that basic and neutral are desirable in this case. Buyers need to be able to envision themselves in a home, and giving them a "blank slate" of neutral colors is a great way to do that.

13. Kitchen and baths

Kitchens and baths sell homes! Kitchens are often the epicenter of a home because meals are often the central community and relationship building time for couples and families. Kitchens need to have enough storage space for the basic necessity of meal preparation and for bowls, plates, and utensils. Cabinets and countertops are evaluated for their color and design. White cabinets are most popular at this time. The easiest way to update a kitchen is to change out hinges, knobs, and pulls and change the countertops. Farm sinks are growing in popularity. Bathrooms are a basic necessity, but they can also be a luxury. Bathrooms that are too small can make the basic task of getting ready for work or school every day into a chore. However, they can also be a retreat where one can relax and unwind. The difference between the two is immense and is evaluated carefully.

14. Lighting and trim

The lighting and trim possibilities are extremely varied and virtually endless. Lighting (fans and lights) are evaluated for positioning, brightness, color, and finish (brushed nickel and bronze are currently the most popular). Fans are assessed to see if their blade size is proportionate to the room size where they are located. It is very important that the fans, lights, and doorknobs & hinges have matching finishes. This helps create a sense of unity and cohesiveness in the design of a home. Trim includes the knobs and hinges already mentioned as well as the baseboards, door moldings, crown moldings, and specialized ceiling designs (coffered, tray, or vaulted). Taller baseboards and wider moldings are higher end finishes. Vaulted or tray ceilings add value in mid-range homes (up to around $250,000), but are expected in higher priced homes. Coffered ceilings are rare and custom millwork of this sort generally only appears in the finest of homes.

I hope that this information has helped you to start thinking like a buyer. As you can see, there are dozens upon dozens of details to be considered when getting ready to list a home. Just like we all know to take special care of our appearance when we are dating someone and trying to win his/her heart – by getting a haircut, ironing our clothes, putting on our favorite cologne or perfume, and so on – so too must serious home sellers take care to make sure that their home is as presentable and desirable as possible to potential homebuyers. If they don't, then their chances of selling their home at all, and especially for top dollar, fall dramatically. Let me give you two examples in closing.

The High Cost Of Ignoring What Buyers Want

A few years ago I sold a house in the Betton area that had previously sold for $219,000 in 2002. During the boom, its value had risen as high as $400,000. However, during the course of the owner's tenure at the property, several of the major systems began to fail. The roof and plumbing leaked, there were electrical issues, and the AC units were all over 20 years old by the time I listed the house as a short sale. Because of all the major issues with the home (including some cosmetic ones as well), the house ending up selling for a mere $160,000! Can you imagine?! A 2700 square foot house on almost 3/4 of an acre in Betton selling for only $160,000! The new buyers immediately spent over $12,000 on a new roof and plumbing repairs, and have since spent tens of thousands more to upgrade the rest of the home. But, when they're done, they will have increased the property's value significantly. Had the former owner had the means to do those renovations himself, that equity could have been his.

Ironically, the second example is a home that another agent had listed just a few blocks away from the house I just mentioned. It was originally listed in early 2010 for about $350,000. I would drive by that house every few days on my way to the bank. Each time I drove by, I thought, "Wow, they really need to take down some of those trees and put a new roof on that house." This pattern continued for nearly two years. The sellers changed Realtors a few times and the price gradually fell all the way down to $230,000. It sold in October of 2011 for a mere $209,000. And, within a few weeks, guess what the new owners did? That's right; they took down a bunch of trees and installed a new roof. The curb appeal of the house was improved tremendously, and those relatively minor changes have added significant value to the home. Again, the former owners lost out on a lot of equity that could have been theirs.

Don't let these stories be your story.

How To Make Your Home One Of The 40+ I Sell This Year

If you've read this far you may be thinking to yourself that you'd like to work with me to sell your home.

First, let me say...I'm honored you feel that way.

But I need to warn you. I work almost exclusively by referral and will not take on more listings than I can realistically service.

I've sold 95 homes in the last two years and have become one of Tallahassee's top Realtors®. As you can imagine, my plate is quite full. I maintain 15 active listings...and no more.

Why put a limit?

Because you are trusting me with what may be the biggest sale of your life. And you deserve my focused effort to sell your home.

Every week, I'm selling listings so there are regular openings for new listings, but they fill up fast (usually in advance).

If you are ready to list your home and are serious about working with me, I recommend that you complete the application at the back of this guide, and fax or email it to my office.

I'll call you within two business days and let you know if I have openings for new listings...if so, we'll schedule a 1-hour Seller's Consultation at your home.

During this meeting, we'll get to know each other and we'll see if we're a fit. If we are, great, we'll get your house listed and sold as fast as possible!

If you decide I'm not the person for you...no sweat...we'll part as friends, and I'll be happy to refer you to another Realtor® who might meet your needs.

Oh...and there's no cost unless I sell your home.

Don't delay! Send in your application now.

Still Skeptical?

If you're still not sure about my abilities, here are my sales stats as reported by the Tallahassee Board of Realtors.

Keep in mind that I started in real estate at the beginning of the crash and have built one of the top real estate practices FROM SCRATCH, despite the bad economy and the depressed real estate market.

My Sales Stats From
The Tallahassee Board of Realtors

$2.4 million in sales in first 8 months of business.

$4.2 million in sales in 2008 (top 5% of all agents at TBR).

$4.9 million in sales in 2009 (top 3% of all agents at TBR).

$5.2 million in sales in 2010 (top 3% of all agents at TBR).

$5.4 million in sales in 2011 (top 3% of all agents at TBR).

$5.5 million in sales in 2012 (top 3% of all agents at TBR).

$6.8 million in sales in 2013 (top 3% of all agents at TBR).

ABOUT THE AUTHOR

Jason Picht is the most accomplished young Realtor® in the Tallahassee area. After entering the real estate profession in 2007, in the midst of the worst real estate depression in the last 70 years, Jason quickly became a top producing Realtor®, consistently selling over 40 homes a year and ranking among the Top 3% of all agents for five years in a row. He lives in Midtown with his wife Megan and is active in the Tallahassee business community and in his church.

Homeowner's Listing Application

Name: _____

Home Address: _____

Neighborhood: _____

Home Phone: _____ Cell Phone: _____

Email Address: _____

How much do you owe on your home? _____

Why have you decided to sell? _____
_____
_____

How quickly do you need to sell? _____

Who referred you to me? _____

Best day of the week and time for your Seller's Consultation?
M T W TH F (circle one)   Time: _____

Fax to (850) 270-6699 or email to JasonPicht@gmail.com

www.ingramcontent.com/pod-product-compliance
Lightning Source LLC
Chambersburg PA
CBHW070720180526
45167CB00004B/1556